IN PRAISE OF
ESSEX

ESSEX FARM BY JOHN NASH

IN PRAISE OF ESSEX

An Anthology

CHOSEN BY
RONALD BLYTHE

The Alastair Press

Published by
The Alastair Press
2 Hatter Street
Bury St Edmunds
Suffolk

First published 1988

© Selection 1988 by Ronald Blythe

ISBN 1 870567 60 9

Printed in Great Britain by
St Edmundsbury Press Ltd
Bury St Edmunds, Suffolk

Cover photograph: Finchingfield Windmill

Essex

"The vagrant visitor erstwhile,"
  My colour-plate book says to me,
"Could wend by hedgerow-side and stile,
  From Benfleet down to Leigh-on-Sea."

And as I turn the colour-plates
  Edwardian Essex opens wide,
Mirrored in ponds and seen through gates,
  Sweet uneventful countryside.

Like streams the little by-roads run
  Through oats and barley round a hill
To where blue willows catch the sun
  By some white weather-boarded mill.

"A Summer Idyll Matching Tye"
  "At Havering-atte-Bower, the Stocks"
And cobbled pathways lead the eye
  To cottage doors and hollyhocks.

Far Essex, – fifty miles away
  The level wastes of sucking mud
Where distant barges high with hay
  Come sailing in upon the flood.

Near Essex of the River Lea
  And anglers out with hook and worm
And Epping Forest glades where we
  Had beanfeasts with my father's firm.

At huge and convoluted pubs
  They used to set us down from brakes
In that half-land of football clubs
  Which London near the Forest makes.

The deepest Essex few explore
  Where steepest thatch is sunk in flowers
And out of elm and sycamore
  Rise flinty fifteenth-century towers.

I see the little branch line go
  By white farms roofed in red and brown,
The old Great Eastern winding slow
  To some forgotten country town.

Now yarrow chokes the railway track,
  Brambles obliterate the stile,
No motor coach can take me back
  To that Edwardian "erstwhile".

JOHN BETJEMAN. (1954)

THE GREEN DRIVE, EPPING FOREST.

EPPING FOREST

Highly Recommended by Scholars ...

The County of Essex is one of the best situated in this kingdom, on account of its nearness to the capital, conveniency of water-carriage, good roads in general, and other great advantages. This county is not filled with light sands, apt to be blown about with every high wind; nor it is covered with barren rocks, or dreary mountains; but the surface of it is, in general, level. However, it is not dead flat, but diversified with agreeable eminences and fruitful dales ... The country, being inclosed, makes it much more comfortable to live and travel in ... it also makes every man's property, whether great or little, much securer, and more his own, than when it is unfenced, and liable to the encroachments of every joint commoner, or greedy neighbour.

PHILIP MORANT,
The History of Essex (1760–8)

. . . *and Sprites*

Essex is our dower, and greatly doth abound
With every simple good that in the world is found.
. . .
At mighty Neptune's beck, thus ended they their song,
When as from Harwich all the Loving-land along,
Great claps and shouts were heard resounding to the
shore,
Wherewith th'Essexian nymphs applaud their belov'd
Stour.

MICHAEL DRAYTON,
Poly-Olbion (1612 and 1622)

The Lure of the Suburbs

While most commentators were to deplore London's sprawl into rural Essex, the entrepreneurial Daniel Defoe was all for it, insisting that people went to live in the adjacent villages 'not for retirement into the country, but for good company.' He rejoices that:

The village of Stratford, the first in this county from London, is not only increased, but, I believe, doubled; every vacancy filled up with new houses (also) . . . the increase of the value and the rent of the houses formerly standing, has . . . advanced to a very great degree . . . especially on the forest-side, as at Lower-Layton, Layton-Stone, Walthamstow, Woodford, Wansted, and the towns of West-Ham, Plaistow, Upton, etc. In all which places, or near them, above a thousand new foundations have been erected, besides old houses repaired, and all since the Revolution (1688) . . . They tell me that there are no less than two hundred coaches kept by the inhabitants within the circumference of these few villages . . . there are in these villages excellent conversation, and a great deal of it, and that without the mixture of assemblées, gaming houses, and publick foundations of vice and debauchery . . .

DANIEL DEFOE,
A Tour Through England and Wales (1719)

A Perfect Jaunt

Chigwell, my dear fellow, is the greatest place in the world. Name your day for going. Such a delicious old inn opposite the churchyard – and such a lovely ride – such beautiful forest scenery – such an out-of-the-way rural place – such a sexton! I say again, name your day.

CHARLES DICKENS,
Letter to John Forster (1872)

Dickens adored 'London-Essex', alternately built-up and wild, cosily domesticated and sinister, and walked and rode through it all his life.

A Defence of Southend

Mr Woodhouse: 'Ah! there is no end of the sad consequences of your going to South End. It does not bear talking of.'

Mrs John Knightley: 'But why should you be very sorry, sir? – I assure you, it did the children a great deal of good.'

Mr Woodhouse: 'And, moreover, if you must go to the sea, it had better not have been to South End. South End is an unhealthy place. Perry was surprized to hear you had fixed upon South End.'

Mrs John Knightley: 'I know there is such an idea with many people, but indeed it is quite a mistake, sir. – We all had our health perfectly well there, never found the least inconvenience from the mud. . .'

JANE AUSTEN,
Emma (1816)

Clacton is to Southend as a moule marinière is to a winkle.

CLIFFORD BAX,
Highways and Byways in Essex (1939)

The Star

Twinkle, twinkle, little star,
How I wonder what you are!
Up above the world so high,
Like a diamond in the sky.

When the blazing sun is gone,
When he nothing shines upon,
Then you show your little light,
Twinkle, twinkle, all the night.

Then the traveller in the dark,
Thanks you for your tiny spark,
He could not see which way to go,
If you did not twinkle so.

In the dark blue sky you keep,
And often through my curtains peep,
For you never shut your eye,
Till the sun is in the sky.

As your bright and tiny spark,
Lights the traveller in the dark –
Though I know not what you are,
Twinkle, twinkle, little star.

JANE TAYLOR, of Ongar,
The Star (1806)

Bliss

Nothing that I know of can compare with the bosoms of those burnished doves which are Clacton's landladies. They live in houses coloured to match, little houses whose façades have all the chromatic delight of lemon pudding, raspberry sauce, and delicate sweets in blue and green . . . The hub of Clacton is its pier. Walk to the end of this, and there, like as not, you will find the *Laguna Belle*, once known as the *Southend Belle*, and with a history of heroic service in the Dardanelles. She has just brought passengers from London – three glad hours, and it seems not an hour of that supreme and supernal joy which, Swinburne tells us, revives in remembrance the sea-bird's heart in a boy. But the great poet said nothing of the supreme and supernal melancholy if it is the return journey from Clacton you are making, and the joys are left behind.

JAMES AGATE,
Ego 2 (1936)

CLACTON-ON-SEA 1930

Flights of Fancy

Colchester, about the year 1800, was for the young Taylors 'a very Elysium.' There were the Strutts, the Hills, the Stapletons: there was poetry, philosophy, engraving. For the young Taylors were brought up to work hard, and if, after a hard day's toil upon their father's pictures, they had slipped round to dine with the Strutts, they had a right to their pleasure. Already they had won prizes in Darton and Harvey's pocket-book. One of the Strutts knew James Montgomery, and there was talk, at those gay parties, with the Moorish decorations and all the cats ... of printing a joint volume to be called *The Associate Minstrels*, to which James might contribute. The Stapletons were poetical, too. Moira and Bithia would wander over to the old town wall at Balkerne Hill reading poetry by moon-light. Perhaps there was too much poetry in Colchester in 1800 ... One night, when the Taylors had moved to Ongar and old Mr. and Mrs. Taylor were sitting over the fire, there came a knock at the door. Mrs Taylor went down to open it. But who was this sad shabby-looking woman outside? 'Oh, don't you remember the Strutts and the Stapletons, and how you warned me against Captain M.?' cried Fanny Hill, for it was Fanny Hill, poor Fanny Hill, all worn and sunk; poor Fanny Hill, that used to be so sprightly. She was living in a lone house not far from the Taylors, forced to drudge for her husband's mistress, for Captain M. had wasted all her fortune, ruined all her life.

VIRGINIA WOOLF, *The Common Reader, 1st Series* (1925)

COLCHESTER CASTLE BY A. K. GLOVER 1825

Very Special Flowers

John Ray (1627–1705), one of the founders of modern botany, was born at Black Notley, the son of the blacksmith. He was inspired as a boy by the still-fascinating variety of plants to be found in Essex.

Undoubtedly the most interesting plant of Essex is the true or Bardfield oxlip (*Primula elatior*). It is a beautiful primula and ought not to be confounded with the various hybrids between the cowslip and the primrose . . . There are three flowering plants said to be found nowhere else but in special localities in Essex. They are the sickle-leaved hare's ear (*Buphleurum falcatum*) which is abundant in parts of the Ongar district, particularly at Norton Mandeville: the red flowering Fyfield pea (*Lathyrus tuberosus*), found only in cornfields at Fyfield; and a variety of bedstraw (*Galium Vaillenti*), termed small-fruited goose grass, discovered in 1844, and which has spread over a wide district round Saffron Walden, particularly in potato fields.

J. C. COX,
Little Guides, Essex

Candied eringoes – the root of Sea Holly (*Eryngium maritimum*) – were one of Essex's most sought after contributions to the nation's medicine-chest, and sweet-tooth.

Mistress Ford. Sir John! art thou there, my dear, my male deer?

Falstaff. My doe with the black scut! Let the sky rain potatoes; let it thunder to the tune of 'Green Sleeves', hail kissing-comfits and snow eringoes; let there come a tempest of provocation, I will shelter me here.

WILLIAM SHAKESPEARE,
The Merry Wives of Windsor.

Pretty Good Going

The fashion of the Country runs much in long roofes and great cantilevers and peakes . . . From Colchester to Ipswitch and thence to Dedom the way pretty good except 4 or 5 miles they call the Severalls, a sort of deep moore ground and woody; at this place I passed over a wooden bridge pretty large with timber railes of which make they build their bridges in these parts; and now I go into Suffolk which is not so rich land as that part of Essex I passed through which was meadows and grounds with great burdens of grass and corn.

CELIA FIENNES,
Through England on a Side Saddle in the Time of William and Mary (1888)

I love the breakneck hills, that headlong go,
And leave me high, and half the world below.
I love to see the Beech Hill mounting high,
The brook without a bridge and nearly dry.
There's Buckhurst Hill, a place of furze and clouds,
Which evening in a golden blaze enshrouds.
JOHN CLARE, *A Walk in the Forest* (1841)

Essex Brickbats and Wisdom

Braintree for the pure,
Bocking for the poor,
Cogshall for the jeering town, and
Kelvedon for the boor.

Give a Promise,
Live a Promise
Do very well.

Make a Promise,
Break a Promise
Go down to Hell.

'I come not from Heaven, but from Essex.'
WILLIAM MORRIS,
A Dream of John Ball (1888)

Wild Extravagance

This year the poor in the Union-houses of Chelmsford, Halstead, Maldon, and Rochford received an extra allowance on Christmas-day. At Braintree the inmates of the house had roast beef and plum pudding, a pint of strong beer for each adult, half a pint to each child; pipes, tobacco and snuff were also given. Pretty doings at Braintree, truly! At Romford, to the disgrace of the Guardians, the paupers, 400 in number, had 240 plum puddings, weighing in all 600 lbs. What an uproar these proceedings will make at Somerset House. Paupers eating plum puddings on Christmas Day! What will this world come to?

Essex County Standard, January 1st 1841

Feastings

Essex oysters, the matchless 'Colchester Natives' which are now bred in the Pyefleet, the little creek which makes Mersea an island, have been famous as a delicacy for two thousand years.

Ye olde luxuryous Romanes vaunte did mayke,
Of gustfull oisters took in Lucrine's lake;
Your Essex better hath, and suche perchance,
As tempted Cesar first to passe from France.

SIR ASTON COKAYNE,
Poems (1669)

Some parts of the sea shore of Essex yealdeth the best Oysters in England, which are called Walflete oysters; so called of a place in the sea between St. Peter's Chappell and Crowche Creeke, where upon the verie shore was erected a wall for the preservation of the lande. And all the seashore which beateth on that wall is called the Walflete. It is a little full oyster with a verie greene fynn, and like unto this in quantitie and qualitie are none in this lande.

JOHN NORDEN,
Description of Essex (1610)

Divo Claudio Constitutum

The setting up of a temple to the Emperor Claudius in Roman Essex gets short shrift from Seneca and Tacitus, whilst the latter gives the local people, then Trinobantes, high praise. These people had been moved to revolt by their ill treatment by the new colonists and they helped the wife of a neighbouring king, Queen Boadicea, to destroy both the temple and the colony.

'In addition to this – the outraging of the Britishers – the temple dedicated to the divine Claudius was regarded by them as a sort of citadel of eternal domination; also the chosen priests, under pretence of religion, squandered all the money.'

TACITUS,
Annals, Book xiv (c. 90 A.D.)

'Tis but a small matter that Claudius has a temple in Britain, and is worshipped by the barbarians, and addressed as a deity.'
SENECA (4 B.C.–65 A.D.)

'. . . at the age of fifty-one, I suddenly found myself caught in what I may call the 'golden predicament' from which I have never since become disentangled.'
CLAUDIUS in *I, Claudius* by Robert Graves (1934)

The Shakespeare Connection

Fear no more the heat o' the sun,
    Nor the furious winter's rages;
Thou thy worldly task hast done,
    Home art gone, and ta'en thy wages;
Golden lads and girls all must,
As chimney-sweepers, come to dust.

Fear no more the frown o' the great,
    Thou art past the tyrant's stroke:
Care no more to clothe and eat;
    To thee the reed is as the oak:
The sceptre, learning, physic, must
All follow this, and come to dust . . .

This threnody is spoken by the sons of Cymbeline over
the decapitated body of their half-brother Cloten.
Shakespeare's Cymbeline was King Cunobelinus (c. 5
B.C.–43 A.D.) whose capital was Camulodunum
(Colchester), and whose beautiful coins with their
wheat-ear fertility design have been found all over
north Essex. Cymbeline/Cunobelinus linked Celtic
and Roman civilizations, and Shakespeare set his play
as 'Sometimes in Britain, sometimes in Italy.'

Tallyho!

Essex was the chief scene of my sport, and gradually I became known there almost as well as though I had been an Essex squire to the manor born. Few have investigated more closely than I have done the depth and breadth, and water-holding capacities of an Essex ditch. It will, I think, be accorded to me by Essex men generally that I have ridden hard. The cause of my delight in the amusement I have never been able to analyse to my own satisfaction. In the first place I know very little about hunting – though I know very much of the accessories of the field. I am too blind to see hounds turning, and cannot therefore tell whether the fox has gone this way or that. Indeed, all the notice I take of hounds is not to ride over them. My eyes are so constituted that I can never see the nature of a fence. I either follow someone, or ride at it with the full conviction that I may be going into a horse-pond or a gravel-pit . . . I am very heavy and have never ridden expensive horses . . . But I ride still after the same fashion, and with a boy's energy, determined to get ahead . . .

ANTHONY TROLLOPE,
Autobiography (1883)

Something To Boast About

This is a good country. Where else are lanes so winding, nightingales so tame, kingcups so yellow, bluebells so blue? ... And what other district in the whole of England has been favoured by a visit from a Dragon?

This is not romance. It happened in 1405. John of Trokelowe and Henry of Blandforde have left an account (*Chronica Monasterii* S. Albani) in monkish Latin which ranks as a first-class piece of reporting. Recently, they say, at the village of Bures near Sudbury a dragon appeared, *vastus corpore, cristato capite, dente serrato, cauda protensa, nimia longitudine,** which did evil by going to and fro among the sheep, killing many. At which the bowmen of Richard de Waldegrave, knight, on whose land the dragon lurked, moved out; but the body of the dragon turned the arrows side, and they sprang back from its armour as if from stone or iron; and those arrows which fell on the spine of its back glanced off again, as if they had struck plates of bronze. Whereupon the whole countryside was aroused. But when the dragon saw that the bowmen were advancing again to the attack it took refuge in the mere at Wormingford and hid among the reeds; nor was it seen any more.

*Vast in body, with a tufted head, saw-like teeth and a tail immeasurably long.

THOMAS WOOD,
True Thomas (1936)

Edward the Confessor puts Ranulph Peperkin in charge of an Essex Hundred

Ich Edward Koning,
Have yeven of my forest the keeping
Of the hundred of Chelmer and Dancing
To Ranulph Peperkin and his kindling,
With harte and hinde, doe and bocke,
Hare and foxe, catt and broche,
Wilde fowell with his flocke,
Partrich, fesant hen and fesant cock,
With greene and wilde stob and stock;
To kepen and to yemen by all her might
Both by day and eke by night.

WILLIAM CAMDEN,
Britannia (1586)

The Poet Gives his Daughter Havering-atte-Bower

What shall I give my daughter the younger
More than will keep her from cold and hunger?
I shall not give her anything.
If she shared South Weald and Havering,
Their acres, the two brooks running between,
Paine's Brook and Weald Brook,
With pewit, woodpecker, swan and rook,
She would be richer than the queen
Who once on a time sat in Havering Bower
Alone, with the shadows, pleasure and power.
She could do no more with Samarcand,
Or the mountains of a mountain land
And its far white house above cottages
Like Venus above the Pleiades.
Her small hands I would not cumber
With so many acres and their lumber,
But leave her Steep and her own world
And her spectacled self with hair uncurled,
Wanting a thousand little things
That time without contentment brings.

EDWARD THOMAS,
Collected Poems (1920)

Appreciated Lots

In the much defamed County of Essex I gleaned the first rudiments of my professional education, and as early impressions are the most durable, I still feel a strong predilection for the pleasant sunny vales, primrose banks, and shady dingles, where the careless years of youth passed merrily along.

Mersea Island is full of tradition, tumuli, tessellated pavements, and Roman remains; Praetors have here planted their Eagles; the Count of the Saxon Shore, a mighty monster in his day, resided here, and some thousand years ago, the great Alfred pitched his tent in these unwholesome regions.

St John's Abbey and St Botolph's Priory at Colchester, will soon be Mac-Adam-ized.

At Borham the Ratcliffs crowd in mouldering pomp.

At Theydon Mount the Smyths lie in profusion and confusion, and in attitudes and attire martial, civil, devotional and funeral.

Professional Excursions by an Auctioneer (1843)

Change-ringing is a great and brilliant passion in Essex. The first peal ever rung in the county was at Saffron Walden on Christmas Day, 1753, and the town holds a 'Great Ringing Day' every 27th June. The following is the record of the first peal:

To inform all Lovers and Professors of the Art of Ringing that the Society of young Ringers of this town, on Tuesday, the 25th December last, being Christmas-Day, did ring the true Peal of Grandsire Triples, composed of 148 Bobs, and two singles, which they effected in three hours and twenty minutes; and on Tuesday following, being New-Year's-Day, they compleated the same in eight minutes less than before (being the only times the same has been rung there since there has been eight bells) to the no small mortification of their antagonists (some of the Old Society), who instead of instruction gave them all the obstruction in their power . . .

By the end of the 18th century the Saffron Walden ringers had achieved such heights that it was said, 'the striking was so excellent as not to attract the musical ear but to enrapture the susceptible heart.'

The time draws near the birth of Christ;
   The moon is hid, the night is still;
   A single church below the hill
Is pealing, folded in the mist.

A single peal of bells below,
   That wakens at this hour of rest
   A single murmur in the breast,
That these are not the bells I know.

Like strangers' voices here they sound,
   In lands where not a memory strays,
   Nor landmark breathes of other days,
But all is new unhallow'd ground.

These celebrated lines from Alfred Tennyson's *In Memoriam* (1850) were written at High Beech, Epping, which was 'new unhallow'd ground' because the poet's friend Arthur Hallam had not been there. The 'single church below the hill' whose 'single peal of bells' he hears is Waltham Abbey.

Glorious Thaxted

Standing in those empty aisles, and seeing the shafts of sunlight slanting through the pillars, Holst dreamed of a festival of music that might happen there one day. He would bring down his pupils, past and present, from Morley College and St. Paul's Girls' School, and they would do 'Sleepers Wake' and 'Soul, Array Thyself,' and Palestrina, and Vittoria and Purcell.

After the first festival of Whitsun, 1916, Holst wrote to a friend, 'It *was* a feast – an orgy. Four whole days of perpetual singing and playing, either properly arranged in the church or impromptu in various houses or still more impromptu in ploughed fields during thunder-storms, or in the train going home.

In the intervals between the services people drifted into the church and sang motets or played violin or 'cello. And others caught bad colds through going long walks in the pouring rain singing madrigals and folk songs and rounds the whole time.'

IMOGEN HOLST,
Gustav Holst (1938)

Summer Magic

. . . . The loveliest forest in the world – not equal to
what it was, but still the loveliest forest in the world,
and the pleasantest, especially in summer; for it is then
thronged with grand company, and the nightingales,
and cuckoos, and Romany chals and chies (boys and
girls). As for the Romany-chals there is not such a place
for them in the whole world as the Forest. Them that
wants to see Romany-chals should go to the Forest,
especially to the Bald-Faced Hind on the hill above
Fairlop, on the day of Fairlop Fair. It is their trysting-
place, as you would say, and there they musters from
all parts of England, and there they whoops, dances,
and plays, keeping some order, nevertheless, because
the Rye of all the Romans is in the house, seated behind
the door.

GEORGE BORROW,
Romany Lavo-Lil Word-book of the Romany,
or English Gipsy Language. (1874)

The Essex Thames flows to the Congo

We felt meditative, and fit for nothing but placid staring. The day was ending in a serenity of still and exquisite brilliance. The water shone pacifically; the sky, without a speck, was a benign immensity of unstained light; the very mist on the Essex marshes was like a gauzy and radiant fabric, hung from the wooded rises inland, and draping the low shores in diaphanous folds . . . The old river in its broad reach rested unruffled at the decline of the day, after ages of good service done to the race that peopled its banks, spread out in the tranquil dignity of a waterway leading to the uttermost parts of the earth.

(Conrad, who lived in Essex for some years, then imagines this scene as it could have appeared to a Roman commander sailing along the edge of Essex.) 'Sandbanks, marshes, forests, savages – precious little to eat fit for a civilized man, nothing but Thames water to drink. No Falernian wine here, no going ashore. Here and there a military camp lost in the wilderness . . . cold, fog, tempests, disease, exile and death . . .'

JOSEPH CONRAD,
Heart of Darkness (1902)

The Conversion of the East Saxons

My house is in the plains beyond the mouth of Thames
And built by the rushing wind and the tongued flames
Where the coast of Heaven borders the Essex coast,
And the byres of Essex are the shires of the Holy Ghost.
I am as old as the whole church in Britain.
Cedd raised the first rough fold of my sheep . . .
I was with holy Aidan, come from Iona
Lord of Lindisfarne in the spiritual land . . .
I was sent by him to lead a raid into Essex.
I obeyed. Forest and ford heard the sound
Of the northern sea of Christ crying, Alleluia!
So there we stamped the sacraments on them.
At Maldon and Tilbury I made a house of monks
To be hosts of adoration . . .

CHARLES WILLIAMS,
The Judgement of Chelmsford (1935)

The Dunmow Oath – Essex's immortal contribution to marital happiness

You shall swear, by custom of concession,
That you ne'er made nuptial transgression;
Nor since you were married Man and Wife,
By household brawls or contentious strife,
Or otherwise, in bed or at board,
Offended each other in deed or in word;
Or since the parish clerk said Amen,
Wished yourselves unmarried agen;
Or in a twelvemonth and a day
Repented not in thought any way,
But continued true in thought and desire
As when you joined hands in holy quire;
If to these conditions without all fear
Of your own accord you will freely swear,
A whole Gammon of Bacon you shall receive
And bear it hence with love and good leave.
For this is our Custom at Dunmow well known,
Though the Pleasure be ours, the Bacon's your own.

THE DUNMOW FLITCH PROCESSION

Brief Encounters

I took notice of a strange decay of the sex here (the Essex marshes) insomuch that it is very frequent to meet with men that had from five or six to fourteen or fifteen wives, nay, and some more . . . The reason as a merry fellow told me was this: that they, being bred in the marshes themselves and seasoned to the place, did pretty well, but that they always went up into the uplands for a wife. That when they took the young lasses out of the wholesome, fresh air they were healthy, but they presently changed complexion, got an ague or two, and seldom held it above half a year, or a year at most. 'And then,' said he, 'we go to the uplands again and fetch another.' So that marrying of wives was reckoned a kind of farm to them.

DANIEL DEFOE,
A Tour Through Great Britain (1722)

In a Manner of Speaking

The dialect spoken by the lower and middle-classes in Essex is marked by a combination of a drawl and a nasal twang, which is anything but pleasant to an educated ear . . . It is asserted that nearly one half of *Gammer Gurton's Needle* (1575) is written in the Essex dialect . . . It retains much of the original Saxon. The Essex peasant and yeoman also use the strong instead of the weak form in the past tenses of verbs. Thus he will say that he *rep* (reaped) an acre of wheat, that he *sew* (sowed tares in the field, and *mew* (mowed) them after; that he *holp* (helped) to load the wagon, that when *lod* (laden) he *dreff* (drove) it off . . .

EDWARD WALFORD,
A Tourist's Guide to Essex (1882)

I have been told, and I heard it without surprise, that the manners of the people who live within ten miles of Easton Lodge (the Countess of Warwick's seat near Dunmow) are the best to be found in Essex.

CLIFFORD BAX,
Highways and Byways in Essex (1939)

Inspiring Scenes

By the 1920s Britain's two most popular novelists had established their homes in Essex and were living in the county in high style, H. G. Wells at Little Easton (6 bathrooms) and Arnold Bennett at Thorpe-le-Soken (butlers and yachts). Here is Bennett on a visit to Wells:

Sunday, 7 November 1926. A lovely, a heavenly morning; very clear and sunshiny. But very damp underfoot. I breakfasted with Jane Wells at 9.15 and then the others came down. Then H.G. and I and D. went for a walk in Easton Park and the grounds of Easton Lodge, and saw a heron on the lake . . . We came back, and H.G. and I changed, and all six of us played ball games for 50 minutes. Fine lunch with 3 ducks and a hot apple pie. After which, sleep, which enabled me to miss tennis. There was some tennis and some bridge and some Schubert trio on the gramophone, and some yacht talk, and some tea – with rose leaf jam . . . H.G. disappeared for about 90 minutes after tea. We thought he was reading or asleep. But at midnight he told us that he had suddenly had the ideas for continuing a novel that he hadn't touched for a month, and so had gone on with it.

ARNOLD BENNETT,
The Journals, Selected and Edited by Frank Swinnerton (1933)

Superior to Surrey

Surrey is full of rich stockbrokers, company-promoters, bookies, judges, newspaper proprietors. Sort of people who fence the paths across their parks ... Surrey people are not properly English at all. They are strenuous. You have to get on or get out. They drill their gardeners, lecture very fast on agricultural efficiency, and have miniature rifle ranges in every village. It's a county of new notice-boards and barbed-wire fences; there's always a policeman round the corner. They dress for dinner, They dress for everything ... And they lock up their churches on a week-day ... Now here in Essex we're as lax as the eighteenth century. We hunt in any old clothes. Our soil is a rich succulent clay; it becomes semi-fluid in winter – when we go about in waders shooting duck. All our finger-posts have been twisted round by facetious men years ago. And we pool our breeds of hens and pigs. Our roses and oaks are wonderful; that alone shows that this is the real England. If I wanted to play golf – which I don't, being a decent Essex man – I should have to motor ten miles into Hertfordshire. And for rheumatics and longevity Surrey can't touch us.

H. G. WELLS,
Mr Britling Sees it Through (1916)

Once Upon a Time

The opening words of what was for three generations of Essex people their favourite tale. Many girls were named after its heroine. The author was the rector of East Mersea in the 1870s.

Between the mouths of the Blackwater and the Colne, on the east coast of Essex, lies an extensive marshy tract veined and freckled in every part with water. At high tide the appearance is that of a vast surface of Sargasso weed floating on the sea, with rents and patches of shining water traversing and dappling it in all directions. The creeks, some of considerable length and breadth, extend many miles inland, and are arteries whence branches out a fibrous tissue of smaller channels, flushed with water twice in twenty-four hours. At noontides, and especially at the equinoxes, the sea asserts its royalty over this vast region, and over-flows the whole, leaving standing out of the flood only the long island of Mersea, and the lesser islet, called the Ray. This latter is a hill of gravel rising from the heart of the marshes, crowned with ancient thorn-trees, and possessing, what is denied the mainland, an unfailing spring of purest water.

. . . A more desolate region can scarcely be conceived, and yet it is not without beauty . . . When all vegetation ceases to live, and goes to sleep, the marshes are alive and wakeful with countless wild fowl. At all times they are haunted with sea mews and roysten crows; in winter they teem with wild duck and grey geese.

SABINE BARING-GOULD,
Mehalah: A Story of the Salt Marshes (1880)

A Flood-tide Fit for Heroes

It was an unknown Essex poet who has left us with the magnificent *Battle of Maldon*, an epic made up of nine brave speeches spoken by Byrhtnoth and his warriors as they attempted to halt the advance of the Danes across the River Blackwater in August 991. The causeway where it was fought can still be seen. Old and brave, Byrhtnoth shouts across the water,

'Listen, messenger! Take back this reply:
Tell your people the unpleasant tidings
That over here there stands a noble earl with his troop –
Guardians of the people and of the country,
The home of *Ethelred*, my prince – who'll defend this
land
To the last ditch. We'll sever the heathens' heads
From their shoulders. It would be much to our shame
If you took our tribute* and embarked without battle
Since you've intruded so far
And so rudely into this country.
No! You'll not get your treasure so easily.
The spear's point and the sword's edge, savage battle-
play,
Must teach us first that we have to yield tribute.'
Then *Byrhtnoth* gave word that all his warriors should
walk
With their shields to the river bank.

Translated by Kevin Crossley-Holland
*Dane-geld

MALDON 1830

The 'Old People'

This Essex coast breeds a strange, fierce love of itself. It is a country for men who love solitude and the silence of the sea. Its own men, the fishermen and the fowlers, the winklers and shepherds, the bargemen and the marsh 'lookers', with here and there still an ancient with gold rings in his ears and still in quiet creek-head villages, 'wise women' who will charm your warts away and cure your cows, these people are a race apart. They are the authentic salt of the earth, as salty in mind, as bracing in speech as the sea-verges which nursed them. They are supreme individualists, fierce in independence, polite with nature's own courtesy and witty with the spontaneous wit which puts the towns-man's thought-out reiterated jokes to shame.

J. WENTWORTH-DAY,
Coastal Adventure (1949)

Out in the quiet, remote villages in Essex, the years pass easily . . . The little children who toddle after their mother while she gathers wood for firing or goes gleaning among the stubble, grow to be useful helpers with the beasts in the yard or with horses at the plough: they drive the geese, or tend sheep, or learn to thatch. Some go and follow careers in the greater world at Colchester or Chelmsford. But mostly they remain until the years sap their vigour, and give them endurance and stoicism as to present and future . . . Work slowly becomes more onerous; the ageing women pick the stones from the fields for the last time, the men go for the last day's hedging . . .

JESSE BERRIDGE,
The Tudor Rose (1925)

A Revelation

. . . I have been absent from this place (East Bergholt) for more than a fortnight, on a visit to the Rev. Mr Driffield at Feering near Kelvedon. He is a very old friend of my father's, and once lived in this parish. He has remembered me for a long time; as he says he christened me one night in great haste, about eleven o'clock. Some time ago I promised him a drawing of his house and church at Feering, and during my visit, he had occasion to go to visit his living at Southchurch, and I was very happy to embrace his offer of accompanying him; by which I saw more of the county of Essex than I had ever before, and the most beautiful part of it; as I was at Maldon, Rochford, South End, Hadleigh, Dansbury, etc. . . .

At Hadleigh there is a ruin of a castle, which from its situation is a really fine place. It commands a view of the Kent hills, the Nore, and the north foreland, and looking many miles out to sea . . . I have filled, as usual, a little book of hasty memorandums of the places which I saw . . .

John Constable to his fiancée Maria Bicknell, July 3rd., 1814. Many years later, mourning her death, he returned to this place to paint the tragic and magnificent *Hadleigh Castle*.

A Commitment

It was in Essex that Dr Samuel Johnson, aged 54, and James Boswell, aged 23, were to cement their famous friendship. Having met a few weeks earlier, Johnson insisted upon accompanying young Boswell on the stage-coach to Harwich, where the latter was to sail for Holland. They set out on 5th August, 1763.

Next day we got to Harwich to dinner . . . We went and looked at the church, and having gone into it and walked up to the altar, Johnson, whose piety was constant and fervent, sent me to my knees, saying, 'Now that you are going to leave your native country, recommend yourself to the protection of your Creator and Redeemer . . .

My revered friend walked down with me to the beach, where we embraced and parted with tenderness, and engaged to correspond with letters. I said, 'I hope, Sir, you will not forget me in my absence.' Johnson. 'Nay, Sir, it is more likely you should forget me, than that I should forget you.' As the vessel put out to sea, I kept my eyes upon him for a considerable time, while he remained rolling his majestic frame in his usual manner; and at last I perceived him walk back into the town, and he disappeared.

Boswell's *Life of Johnson* (1791)

The Roothing

The Roothing river runs through the eight parishes called High Roothing, Aythorpe Roothing, White Roothing, Leaden Roothing, Margaret Roothing, Abbots Roothing, Berners Roothing and Beauchamp Roothing, and so into the Thames. Large ships take ten years to sail from its mouth to Chapel End, where it rises. The narrowest part of the River is so wide that two men cannot see across it. There is a ferryboat going between Woodbury and Clayford, but the journey is so long that it has not yet reached the other side. . . .

There are many farms in the Roothings where the grain and the fruits grow to a great size. An ear of corn is there too large to be threshed with flails: each grain has to be dragged from the ear by a team of horses and then sawn into quarters in a sawmill before being ground . . . In the Autumn the harvesters are very busy gathering the fruit of the currant trees, but the work is very dangerous: twelve new labourers were one day standing under one of the trees, when a red currant fell on their heads and killed them. The farmers suffer greatly from the bees, which often carry off their stacks of sweet hay in mistake for pollen dust . . . The butterflies there have wings as large as the mainsail of a ship, and the draught made by the many butterflies which fly near the River is very useful to sailors, who avail themselves of these winds – called by them 'the butter winds' – to sail their huge carracks, laden with the produce of the Roothings, to the most distant countries.

There is a lake in Topping which is a hundred miles long and fifty miles wide and twenty miles deep, but the folk of Woodbury drink so heartily that there is never more than a few hundred fathoms of water in it. Because the lake is so shallow there is no room in it for any fish except lemon-soles, of which there are two which cover the entire bed. The movements of these fish cause the earthquakes that are so common in America.

The church at Woodbury has an unusually high steeple: not long after it was built it knocked a chip out of the moon as it was passing, but the gap allows the moon to pass comfortably now.

In thick weather the lambs are made to bray on the top of Yardley Hill to warn the ships coming up the Thames.

EDWARD AND GUNNAR JOHNSTON.

When the world was made, the Roothings were first made, then all the rest was added.

Old Essex saying.

Acknowledgements

I am most grateful to the following for their kind permission to quote from copyright material: to John Murray for *Essex* by Sir John Betjeman, to Macmillan for extracts from Clifford Bax's *Highways and Byways in Essex*, to the Executors of the late James Agate for *Bliss*, to the Hogarth Press for *Flights of Fancy*, to Arthur Barker for a sentence from Robert Graves's *I, Claudius*, to the Executors of the late Dr Thomas Wood for *Something to Boast About*, to the Executors of the late Imogen Holst for *Glorious Thaxted*, to Oxford University Press for *The Conversion of the East Saxons*, to Macmillan for *Listen, messenger!*, to Harrap for *Old People*, and to the Librarian of the Essex Collection at Colchester for all his assistance.

The cover photograph of *Finchingfield Windmill* is reproduced by permission of Judges Postcards Ltd.